[redacted]

SHAYKH ʿABD AL-RAḤMĀN AL-SAʿDĪ
(*d.*1376H/1956CE)

al-durrat al-fākhirah

THE EXQUISITE PEARL

TRANSLATION:
ABU AALIYAH SURKHEEL SHARIF

THE JAWZIYYAH PRESS

British Library Cataloguing in Publishing Data
A catalogue record of this book is available from the British Library.
ISBN: 0 9542166 0 1

TITLE: The Exquisite Pearl
AUTHOR: ʿAbd al-Raḥmān al-Saʿdī
FIRST EDITION: Ṣafr 1423H/ April 2002CE

PUBLISHED BY:
The Jawziyyah Press
P.O.Box 38704
London E.11 3WH
United Kingdom

e-mail: sales@jawziyyah.com
Website: www.jawziyyah.com

PRINTED BY:
Impeks Publishing
1st Floor Suite
197 Cranbrook Road
Ilford, Essex 1G1 4TA
Tel: 020 8518 3433
United Kingdom

TABLE *of* CONTENTS

Translator's Preface v
About the Book xv
Arabic Text of the Poem xxii
Translation of the Poem xxvi

Introduction 1
The Awakening 2
The Aspiration 4
The Station of Sincerity 5
The Station of Fear and Hope 7
The Station of Love 9
The Station of Remembrance 11
Seeking Nearness to Allāh 14
Self-Inspection 15
The Station of Patience 16
The Station of Contentment 18
The Station of Gratitude 20
The Station of Reliance 22
The Station of Excellence 24
The Station of Good Character 26
The Station of Attentive Care 28
The Station of Renunciation 30
The Fellowship 32

Translator's Bibliography 35
General Index 36

TRANSLATOR'S PREFACE

ALL PRAISE BE TO ALLĀH, Lord of the worlds. May Allāh extol and shower abundant blessings and peace upon the best of His creation, the Prophet Muḥammad; and upon his Family, his Companions and all who follow them until the Day of Resurrection.

To continue:

The Material Landscape

Allāh, Exalted is He, said in the Majestic Qur'ān:

> Whoever aspires to the harvest of the Afterlife, We grant him increase in his harvest; and whoever aspires to the harvest of this world, We grant him of it here, but in the Afterlife he shall have no portion. [al-Shūrā 42:20]

In today's maelstrom of materialism and spread of licentious western liberalism, most people's aspirations tend not to extend beyond those of gratifying their desires and appeasing the urges of their appetites. That inner yearning within the human condition to know our origins and our Creator, to understand the purpose of our existence, to bring into our lives a richer and deeper sense of meaning, has - for all intents and purposes - been stifled or turned into a social taboo. In short, those 'fundamental' questions and inner yearnings that ultimately define our humanity have, in most cases, been either suppressed and ignored by the individuals, or methodically purged from them!

The result: greed, selfishness, nihilism, and spiritual bankruptcy have become dominant hallmarks of many of today's individuals; whereas, hedonism, mass-consumerism, environmental vandalism and rape of the earth's natural resources so as to ensure today's material comforts, perks and profits, have become emblematic of humanity at a more global level. It would seem that though the ideology of materialism has aided people in their actual quality of living, it nevertheless continues to play havoc with their actual quality of life!

Caught up in this milieu is the Muslim world. Betaken with western culture, the sole pre-occupation for many Muslims has now become 'the standard of living' and their own material advancement. As such, the Muslim world has fallen prey to a similar dysfunctionality and dissonance that inevitably occurs when faith, spirituality and conformity to the Divine Will are neglected, and materialism is embraced. The Prophet Muḥammad *ṣallallāhu 'alayhi wa sallam,* forewarned: "By Allāh! It is not poverty that I fear for you, but I fear the world will be opened to you as it was opened to those before you, and that you would compete with one another over it as they competed, and that it would destroy you as it destroyed them."[1]

The Sound Aspiration

Disengaging from this malady of materialism requires engaging the higher purpose for which we were created, the prelude to which is sound aspiration (*irādah*). What is meant by 'sound aspiration' is the desire to draw closer to Allāh through inner struggle, or *mujāhadah;* in other words it is the heart's quest for its spiritual sustenance. Imām Ibn al-Qayyim, may Allāh have mercy upon him, explained: 'The signs of sound aspiration is that the aspirant's main concern lies in pleasing his Lord, preparing to meet Him, being grieved at the times he spent in other than his Lord's pleasure, and regretting the missed opportunities

1. Recorded by al-Bukhārī (no.1465) and Muslim (no.1052).

to be close and intimate with Him. The summary of this is that day-in and day-out he has no concern other than this.'[2]

One of the fruits of this aspiration, this 'labour of love,' is that of being granted inner peace. The Prophet, *ṣallallāhu ʿalayhi wa sallam,* said: "Whoever makes the Afterlife his concern, Allāh will gather together his affairs, place contentment in his heart and the world will come to him despite his reluctance; whoever makes the world his concern, Allāh will split-up his affairs, put poverty before him and nothing of the world will come to him except what Allāh has written for him."[3]

The Prophet, *ṣallallāhu ʿalayhi wa sallam,* also said: "Allāh said: O son of Adam! Free yourself for My worship, and I will fill your chest with sufficiency and remove your poverty. But if you do not, I will fill your hands with distraction and will not remove your poverty."[4]

Perhaps the profoundest fruit that arises as a result of this aspiration is being indemnified in Allāh's divine love - as the Prophet, *ṣallallāhu ʿalayhi wa sallam,* said: "Whenever Allāh loves a person, He shelters him from worldliness."[5]

Here the question is often asked: how should material possessions and wealth be dealt with, should they be totally abandoned? The answer to this apparent 'dilemma' was aptly given by Imām Ibn Taymiyyah, may

2. *Al-Fawā'id* (p.171).

3. Recorded by al-Tirmidhī (no.2389) and it was declared to be authentic (*ṣaḥīḥ*) by Shaykh al-Albānī, *Silsilah al-Ṣaḥīḥah* (no.949).

4. Recorded by al-Tirmidhī (no.2466) and others, and it is *ṣaḥīḥ*. Consult: *Silsilah al-Ṣaḥīḥah* (no.1359).

5. Recorded by al-Tirmidhī (no.2036) and Aḥmad, *Musnad* (5/427). It was declared to be *ṣaḥīḥ* by Shaykh al-Albānī, *Ṣaḥīḥ al-Jāmiʿ* (no.282).

Allāh have mercy upon him, who said: 'Wealth should be viewed just like the toilet, in that you have need for it and resort to it when necessary, but it has no place in your heart.'[6]

Our Spiritual Tradition

Islām's Sacred Law, or *sharīʿah,* not only provides guidance for man's external well-being, but it embodies a narrative for his inner growth as well. It is this 'inner' narrative, or spiritual tradition, which guides him to subduing his bestial nature and elevating the angelic nature within his soul, as well as purifying the heart from the spiritual diseases that veil it from knowing Allāh and being truly devoted to Him. Indeed, it is only when the soul transcends its bestiality, and the heart is purified from the veils that render blind its spiritual perception, can one be infused with the illuminations of *iḥsān* - the very essence of faith and spirituality - which the Prophet *ṣallallāhu ʿalayhi wa sallam* explained as being: "That you worship Allāh as if you see Him, for if you do not see Him, He sees you."[7]

Ibn Rajab al-Ḥanbalī, may Allāh have mercy upon him, said as part of his commentary to the above Prophetic words:

'It indicates that the servant (*ʿabd*) should worship Allāh in this manner; namely, evoking the feeling of His nearness and of His being with him as though he sees Him. This in turn necessitates reverence, fear, awe and glorification [of Allāh]; as occurs in the narration of Abū Hurayrah: "That you revere Allāh as if you see Him." It also necessitates sincerity in worship, as well as exerting all one's efforts in improving, completing and perfecting it.'[8]

---

6. *Majmūʿ Fatāwā* (10/663).

7. Recorded by al-Bukhārī (no.5) and Muslim (no.9).

8. *Jāmiʿ al-ʿUlūm wa'l-Ḥikam* (1/126)

Ibn Rajab further said: 'It has been said that it [the second part of the sentence] is the cause for the first part. This is because when the servant is ordered to have vigilance (*murāqabah*) of Allāh whilst worshipping Him and to feel His closeness, to the point that it is as if he was seeing Him, then this may be difficult. So he seeks aid to attain this through his faith that Allāh sees him, is fully aware of his secret and public [acts], his inner and outer [states], and that nothing of his affairs is ever hidden from Him. When he actualises this station (*maqām*), it becomes easier for him to move to the second station, which is where there is a continual realisation, upon spiritual perception (*baṣīrah*), of Allāh's closeness to His servant and of His being with him; to the extent that it is as if he actually sees Him.

It has further been said: Rather, it refers to the fact that whosoever finds it difficult to worship Allāh as if seeing Him, then he should worship Allāh upon the realization that Allāh sees him and is fully aware of what he is doing. So let him feel shy of Allāh due to the Divine gaze over him; as one of the gnostics (*'ārifūn*) said: 'Fear Allāh, lest He becomes [to you] the most despised of those watching you.' Another said: 'Fear Allāh in proportion to His power over you, and feel shy of Allāh in proportion to His closeness to you.' A female gnostic from the Predecessors (*salaf*) said: 'Whoever acts for Allāh, due to witnessing Allāh (*mushāhadah*), is a gnostic (*'ārif*); whoever acts for Allāh, due to knowing that Allāh sees him, is sincere (*mukhliṣ*).' So this indicates the two stations that were previously mentioned:

The First: the station of sincerity (*ikhlāṣ*), which is where the servant acts whilst bringing to mind that Allāh observes him, that Allāh is fully conversant with whatever he is doing, and that Allāh is close to him. So when the servant brings this to mind in his actions - this being the root of his actions - then he is sincere to Allāh. This is because evoking this feeling during his actions prevents him from turning to other than Allāh, or from desiring other than Him in his actions.

The Second: the station of *mushāhadah.* This is where the servant acts whilst witnessing Allāh with his heart; which is when the heart is so illuminated by faith, and the spiritual perception is so heightened, it is as if the unseen is beheld with one's eyes.'[9]

The Required Wayfaring

So when love of Allāh stirs in the heart and the winds of yearning for the Afterlife (*ākhirah*) diffuse throughout the soul, then striving (*jihād*) against whatever hinders wayfaring (*sulūk*) to Allāh becomes essential, in order to nurture this 'awakening.' Allāh, Exalted is He, said:

> As for those who strive in Us, We shall guide them to Our paths. [al-ʿAnkabūt 29:69]

Commenting upon this verse, Ibn al-Qayyim, may Allāh have mercy upon him, said: 'Allāh, Transcendant is He, made guidance dependant upon *jihād.* The most perfect of people with regards guidance are those that perform *jihād* the most. The most obligatory *jihād* is the *jihād* against the ego (*nafs*), capriciousness (*hawā*), the Devil (*shayṭān*), and the world (*dunyā*). Whoever wages *jihād* for Allāh's sake against these four, Allāh will guide to the paths of His good pleasure, which in turn lead to His Paradise. Whoever leaves *jihād,* forfeits guidance in proportion to what he leaves of it.'[10]

So a vital aspect of a servant's *sulūk* is engaging in an inner struggle in order to attain a deep conviction in the *sharīʿah* truths, remove sluggishness, make compliance with its rules easy and spontaneous, and to eradicate the ego's opposition. Put simply, it is to carry out the *sharīʿah* commands, persevere in it, and to do so sincerely and with presence of

9. *Jāmiʿ al-ʿUlūm wa'l-Ḥikam* (1/128-129).

10. *Al-Fawāʾid* (p.91).

heart. Furthermore: '*Sulūk* is,' as Ibn Taymiyyah explained: 'of two types: [Firstly] the *sulūk* of the Righteous (*abrār*), the companions of the right hand, which is fulfilling what is obligatory and forsaking what is forbidden, both inwardly and outwardly. Secondly, the *sulūk* of the Ones Brought Near (*muqarrabūn*), the fore-runners, which involves fulfilling the obligatory and the recommended, as best as possible, and leaving the forbidden and the disliked.'[11]

The Prophet *ṣallallāhu 'alayhi wa sallam* said: "Allāh, Exalted is He, said: Whoever shows enmity to a friend of Mine, I shall be at war with him. My servant does not draw closer to Me with anything more beloved to Me than the religious duties I have obligated upon him, and My servant continues to draw closer to Me with voluntary deeds so that I love him. When I love him, I am his hearing with which he hears; his seeing with which he sees; his hand with which he strikes; and his foot with which he walks."[12]

Once again we are returned to the station of *iḥsān,* as Ibn Rajab, may Allāh have mercy upon him, explained:

'Whenever a person strives in drawing closer to Allāh, Exalted is He, by [performing] the obligatory deeds, then the optional ones, Allāh draws him closer to Himself and raises him from the degree of faith to that of *iḥsān.* Here he begins to worship Allāh, witnessing His presence and having vigilance, as if he sees Him. His heart fills with gnosis of Allāh, and with love, reverence, fear, grandeur, awe, intimacy and yearning of Him - to the extent that the heart is so filled with gnosis of Him, that it sees Him with the eye of spiritual perception.'[13]

11. *Majmū' Fatāwā* (19/274).

12. Recorded by al-Bukhārī (no.6502).

13. *Jāmi' al-'Ulūm wa'l-Ḥikam* (2/345-346).

Finally, as the servant embodies and internalises obedience to Allāh, and as his spirit is elevated and his ego debased, he is filled with a deep concern for people's welfare and for being in their service; aiding, guiding, counselling, and supplicating for them. It is here, in the absence of the ego, that the effusions of true altruism pour forth from the servant, exemplifying the Prophetic concern and conduct.

The Blissful Life

The Prophet *ṣallallāhu ʿalayhi wa sallam* said: "He has relished the taste of faith who is pleased with Allāh as Lord, with Islām as Religion, and with Muḥammad as Messenger."[14]

He *ṣallallāhu ʿalayhi wa sallam* also said: "There are three things which, if they are present in anyone, will cause him to taste the sweetness of faith: that Allāh and His Messenger are more beloved to him than all else; that he loves others only for the sake of Allāh; and that he should hate to revert to disbelief after Allāh has saved him from it, just as he would hate to be cast into a blazing fire."[15]

The heart, when it is truly sincere in its servitude (*ʿubūdiyyah*) to Allāh, is given to taste such sweetness, and experience such delight, that nothing besides this servitude is held more beloved to it. For the spiritually sound heart finds nothing sweeter, more blissful, or gratifying to it than the sweetness of faith (*īmān*), which is born out of the labours of its gnosis, love and servitude to Allāh, Blessed and Exalted is He. Imām Ibn Taymiyyah, may Allāh have mercy upon him, said:

'If you do not find the deed producing a sweetness or expansion in your heart, then blame it. For the Lord, Exalted is He, is indeed appreciative.'

14. Recorded by Muslim (no.34).

15. Recorded by al-Bukhārī (no.21) and Muslim (no.43).

Meaning that He will reward the doer of the deed in this world with experiencing sweetness, expansion and delight in his heart. Whenever one does not find this occurring, then the deed is defective.[16]

Imām Ibn al-Qayyim, may Allāh have mercy upon him, elaborated upon this state of bliss and delight experienced by the sincere servant; he said: 'There is no [true] bliss, nor any delight, joy, or completeness for him, except in knowing Allāh, loving Him, being tranquil in the remembrance of Him, feeling delighted in drawing closer to Him and in yearning to meet Him; this being the paradise of the worldly life. Likewise, there is no delight or success for him in the Afterlife, except with his being enveloped in the Abode of Bliss in the Paradise of the next life. So there are for him two paradises, he will not enter the latter without first entering the former.

I heard Shaykh'l-Islām Ibn Taymiyyah, may Allāh sanctify his soul, saying: 'Indeed there is a paradise in this world, whoever does not enter it will not enter the Paradise of the Afterlife.'

One of the gnostics said: 'There are times that pass over the heart about which I say: If the people of Paradise are in the likes of this [state], then what a wonderful life they are in.'

One of the lovers [of Allāh] said: 'The poor people of this world have left it without having tasted the sweetest thing in it.' They asked: What is the sweetest thing in it? He replied: 'Love of Allāh, intimacy with Him, yearning to meet Him, drawing closer to Him, and turning away from everything other than Him,' or words similar to it. Indeed, anyone with life in their heart affirms this and experiences its taste.'[17]

16. Quoted by Ibn al-Qayyim, *Madārij al-Sālikīn* (2/51).

17. *Madārij al-Sālikīn* (1/344).

The Beautific Vision

Allāh, Blessed and Exalted is He, said:

> For those who act with excellence is the greatest good, and even more. [Yūnus 10:26]

This 'greatest good' is a reference to Paradise, whilst this 'even more' is a reference to gazing at the Face of Allāh.[18] For the servant, having lived his life in the pursuit of Allāh's good pleasure and having striven to worship Him in this world as though seeing Him, is then rewarded by Allāh in the Afterlife with Paradise and its delights, the greatest of which is the beautific vision of Allāh. The Prophet of Mercy, *ṣallallāhu 'alayhi wa sallam,* informed us:

"When the people of Paradise enter Paradise and those of Hell enter Hell, a herald shall call out, saying: O people of Paradise! Your Lord has undertaken a promise to you which He wishes to fulfill upon you. They will inquire: 'What might that promise be? Has he not made heavy our scales, whitened our faces, brought us into Paradise and delivered us from Hell?' Then the veil shall be lifted and they shall gaze upon Him. By Allāh! They will not have been given anything more beloved to them than looking at Him."[19]

O Lord! I seek Your forgiveness for speaking about matters for which I am not from its people. O Allāh! We seek refuge in Your pleasure from Your anger; in Your forgiveness from Your chastisement; and in You from You. O Allāh! Grace us with a fervent desire to meet You and with the delight of gazing at Your Face.

---

18. Consult: al-Ṭabarī, *Jāmiʿ al-Bayān ʿan Taʾwīl al-Qurʾān* (6/549); al-Samʿānī, *Tafsīr al-Qurʾān* (2/378-379); al-Baghawī, *Maʿālim al-Tanzīl* (4/130).

19. Recorded by Muslim (no.181).

ABOUT THE BOOK

HERE, THREE ASPECTS OF THE BOOK shall be discussed: its author, its theme, and its translation.

Its Author[20]

The author is ʿAbd al-Raḥmān ibn Nāṣir ibn ʿAbd Allāh ibn Ḥamad al-Saʿdī, from the tribe of Banū Tamīm. He was born on the 12th of Muḥarram, 1307H/1889CE, in the city of ʿUnayzah, situated in the province of al-Qaṣīm; central Saudi Arabia. He was orphaned at a young age; his mother passing away when he was only four, and his father when he was seven. His older brother, Ḥamad, was then entrusted with his care and upbringing.

By the age of twelve Shaykh al-Saʿdī had completed the memorisation of the Qurʾān, after which his pursuit for knowledge of the Sacred Law began in earnest.He studied the traditional disciplines at the hands of a number of senior scholars of the land; from them:

1 - Shaykh Ibrāhīm al-Jāsir. Born in 1241H, he first studied locally, then went to Syria to further his studies. Shaykh Ibrāhīm was well-known for his good manners, scrupulousness and generosity. He was also blessed with a lengthy life, passing away at the age of ninety-seven.

20. This biographical sketch is based upon: al-Ramyān, *al-Juhūd al-Daʿawiyyah wa'l-ʿIlmiyyah li'l-Shaykh ʿAbd al-Raḥmān al-Saʿdī* (pp.15-60).

Under him Shaykh al-Sa'dī studied Qur'ānic exegesis (*tafsīr*), jurisprudence (*fiqh*) and the science of Prophetic traditions (*ḥadīth*).

2 - Shaykh Sāliḥ ibn 'Uthmān al-Qāḍī. Born in 'Unayzah in 1282H, he travelled to Egypt to study at the famous al-Azhar university, where he was granted authorization (*'ijāzah*) in a number of subjects. Under him Shaykh al-Sa'dī studied theology (*tawḥīd*), *tafsīr, fiqh,* fundamentals of jurisprudence (*uṣūl al-fiqh*) and grammar.

3 - Shaykh 'Alī ibn Nāṣir Abū Wādī. He first studied in 'Unayzah and Riyadh, and then travelled to India to study under the *ḥadīth* scholars, obtaining numerous authorizations in this field. Under him Shaykh al-Sa'dī learnt *ḥadīth* and *tafsīr*.

4 - Shaykh 'Abd Allāh ibn 'Ā'iḍ al-Ḥarbī. He was born in 1249H in the city of 'Unayzah. He travelled to the Hijāz province and also to Egypt in his quest for knowledge. From him Shaykh al-Sa'dī learnt *fiqh, uṣūl al-fiqh* and the disciplines connected with the Arabic language.

Shaykh al-Sa'dī, may Allāh have mercy upon him, was known for his worship, character, and abstinence from worldliness. Shaykh Sāliḥ ibn 'Abd al-'Azīz al-'Uthaymīn remarked: 'The deceased - may Allāh have mercy upon him - was exceptional with regards to his excellent conduct and his humility to both young and old. He was a person of worship, abstinence and scrupulousness, as well as a jurist (*faqīh*), traditionalist (*muḥaddith*), exhorter (*wā'iẓ*), orator (*khaṭīb*), linguist and author; he combined within him knowledge of a variety of disciplines.'

Shaykh 'Abd al-'Azīz bin Bāz, may Allāh have mercy upon him, said about him: 'He - may Allāh have mercy upon him - had a great concern for *fiqh* and, in issues involving differences of opinion, paid attention to knowing the stronger opinion along with its respective proof. He hardly spoke unless there was a benefit; I sat with him on more than one occasion in Makkah and Riyadh and he only spoke sparingly, except in issues of knowledge. He was humble and had an excellent character; whoever reads his books will realise his virtue, knowledge and concern for the textual proofs. May Allāh bestow vast mercy upon him.'

From the age of twenty-three, up until his death, the Shaykh devoted his life to teaching, instructing and cultivating the people. During this time he authored over thirty books and treatises; from them:

1 - *Taysīr al-Karīm al-Raḥmān fī Tafsīr Kalām al-Mannān* (Facilitation of the Most-Munificent, Most-Merciful in Explaining the Words of the Most-Benevolent), a concise exegesis of the Qur'ān; simple in its wording, profound in its meanings.

2 - *Al-Tanbīhāt al-Laṭīfah fī mā Iḥtawat 'alayhi'l-'Aqīdah al-Wasiṭiyyah* (The Graceful Awareness of what is Encapsulated in the Creed of al-Wāsiṭiyyah), a brief commentary to Imām Ibn Taymiyyah's treatise on the Muslim creed.

3 - *Manhaj al-Sālikīn wa'l-Tawḍīḥ al-Fiqh fi'l-Dīn* (Methodology of the Wayfarer and an Exposition of the Laws of the Religion), a digest of Ḥanbalī *fiqh*, although in some issues opinions from other *fiqh* schools have been preferred by the Shaykh due to the strength of their proof.

4 - *Irshād Ūl al-Basā'ir wa'l-Albāb li Nayl al-Fiqh* (A Guidance to those Possesing Insight and Understanding for the Attainment of the Law), a compendium of *fiqh* in question and answer form.

5 - *Risālah fi'l-Qawā'id al-Fiqhiyyah* (A Treatise about the Maxims of Jurisprudence), written in poetry form, with brief notes to each line of poetry by the author himself.

6 - *Bahjatu Qulūb al-Abrār* (Delight for the Hearts of the Righteous), a superb exposition of ninety-nine Prophetic traditions that deal with beliefs, manners, morals, *sulūk*, law, and social transactions.

7 - *Al-Wasā'il al-Mufīdah li'l-Ḥayāt al-Sa'īdah* (The Beneficial Means to a Happy Life), in which ways that assist a person in what is now referred to as 'personal and spiritual intelligence,' are discussed.

Shaykh 'Abd al-Raḥmān al-Sa'dī, after suddenly falling ill, passed away just before dawn, on Thursday 23rd of Jumāda al-Ākhir; 1376H. May Allāh shower mercy upon him, be pleased with him, and raise him to the ranks of the Truthful Ones (*al-siddīqūn*).

The Theme

The book consists of a short, didactic poem - which its author entitled: 'The Journey to Allāh and the Home of the Hereafter, or Afterlife (*al-sayr il'allāh wa'l-dār al-ākhirah*) - as well as a brief explanation to the poem, which he called: 'The Exquisite Pearl (*al-durrat al-fākhirah*).' The nature and brevity of the book is such that it may be regarded as an introduction, or a primer, to the science of *sulūk*.

The book elucidates the main stations (*maqāmāt* or *manāzil*) that the heart is required to embrace as part of its journeying to Allāh. What is meant by 'station' is a praiseworthy quality - such as sincerity, love, fear, hope, patience, satisfaction or renunciation - which the heart succeeds in acquiring and firmly rooting in itself. When this occurs, the heart is said to have 'arrived' at that particular station. If, however, the praiseworthy quality wavers and has not settled in it, then the heart is said to be in a state (*ḥāl*), not a station (*maqām*).

Ibn al-Qayyim, may Allāh have mercy upon him, explained the distinction between states and stations in the following manner:

'What is correct here is that these occurrences and stations are named so by taking into consideration the particular state for it. So they are glimmerings (*lawāmi'*), flashes (*bawāriq*) and external appearances (*lawā'iḥ*) at the onset of their occurrence, in the same way that lightening glimmers and flashes from a distance. But when they dawn upon him and he encounters them, then they become states. If they become firmly established within him, without vanishing, then they are called stations. So initially they are glimmers and flashes; midway they are states; and finally they are stations. Therefore, the initial glimmer of light is the state, as well as the station. But these terms are only named so by taking into consideration how they connect with the heart, how manifest they are upon it, and how firmly-rooted they are in it.'[21]

The difference between the two may also be clarified by the following example: Renunciation (*zuhd*) is one of the lofty stations of wayfaring; being proven so by the texts of the Book, the *Sunnah* and the agreement of the Pious Predecessors (*al-salaf al-ṣāliḥ*) of this nation (*ummah*). So knowledge of the world's ephemerality; the censure of it and of those who chase after it; and the praise for those who turn away from it and instead aspire for the Afterlife, is what initially causes the heart to incline towards renunciation. Then, if success is granted, there appears from the limbs certain acts that indicate the presence of this state in the heart, such as shunning worldliness and materialism, and engaging in righteous actions and spiritual works. This state then encounters opposing influences, such as the ego's insinuations, satanic whisperings and the soul's capriciousness, which urge and lure him towards worldliness. In the wake of this onslaught this state may waver or fluctuate; it may even vanish completely. But if these influences are combated, and the effect becomes firmly ingrained and deeply rooted in the heart, then it is called a station.

One of the purposes of *sulūk* is to aid the transition from 'experiencing' states, to 'arriving' at stations; and from experiencing 'moments' of reliance, patience, fear, hope, satisfaction in Allāh, etc., to being 'permanently' adorned with these essential and praiseworthy qualities. The actual vehicle for this transition is inner struggle, or *mujāhadah,* by

21. *Madārij al-Sālikīn* (1/110).

which these qualities may be imposed, and then imprinted, upon the heart. The Prophet, *ṣallallāhu ʿalayhi wa sallam,* said: 'Indeed, knowledge is acquired by learning it, and forbearance is acquired by imposing it [upon oneself].'[22]

About the Translation

The following points are related to the actual translation:

1 - Two critical arabic editions of the book have been used for this translation; the first is the edition of Shaykh ʿAlī Ḥasan al-Ḥalabī,[23] the second is the one prepared by Ashraf ibn ʿAbd al-Maqṣūd;[24] one of the fifteen or so al-Saʿdī titles that he has edited. May Allāh reward them both with goodness for their services and efforts.

2 - Footnotes have been added from the words of Ibn al-Qayyim, a saintly scholar and a master of both the inward and outward sciences of Islām; may Allāh illuminate his grave and sanctify his soul. Most of these words are from his *magnum opus* on Islāmic spirituality, entitled: *Madārij al-Sālikīn* (Stations of the Wayfarers), in which he extensively quotes the pietists and masters of *sulūk* from the early Muslims.

3 - I would like to express my thanks to Safia Debar, Asif Sharif and Arsalan Obaidullah, who proof read the translation and made valuable suggestions for its improvement. I am also grateful to Abu Rumaysah who not only checked the translation, but also contributed immensely in the translation of the actual poetry itself. May Allāh grant each of them felicity and well-being in both worlds.

---

22. Recorded by al-Khaṭīb, *Tārīkh* (9/127). It was declared to be sound (*ḥasan*) by al-Albānī, *Silsilah al-Ṣaḥīḥah* (no.342).

23. Published by Dār Ibn ʿAffān: Khubar; 1418H/1997CE.

24. Published by Aḍwā al-Salaf: Riyadh; 1419H/1998CE.

4 - Headings have been included at the beginning of each chapter. In addition, a bibliography of the sources used for this introduction has been given at the end of this book, along with a general index of names and terms that occur in the book.

Finally

The believer, in his quest for spiritual growth, and in his desire to draw closer to Allāh, knows that his is not a 'one-sided affair.' Rather, he is reassured and comforted by the promise of divine reciprocity, about which the Prophet, *ṣallallāhu 'alayhi wa sallam,* said:

"Allāh, Mighty and Majestic is He, said: I am as My servant thinks I am and I am with him when he remembers Me. If he remembers Me to himself, I remember him to Myself. If he remembers Me in an assembly, I remember him in an assembly better than it. If he draws closer to Me by a hand's span, I draw closer to him by an arm's length; and If he draws closer to Me by an arm's length, I draw closer to him by a fathom; and if he comes walking to me, I come hastening to him."[25]

All praise be to Allāh, Lord of the worlds. May Allāh's blessings and peace be upon our master (*sayyid*), Muḥammad; and upon his Family, his Companions and all those who follow them.

Abu Aaliyah Surkheel ibn Anwar Sharif
8th of Rabīʿ al-Thānī; 1422H
(31st of August, 2001CE)
London, England

25. Recorded by al-Bukhārī (no.7405) and Muslim (no.2675).

ARABIC TEXT OF THE POEM

سَعِدَ الَّذِينَ تَجَنَّبُوا سُبُلَ الرَّدَى
وَتَيَمَّمُوا لِمَنَازِلِ الرِّضْوَانِ

فَهُمُ الَّذِينَ أَخْلَصُوا فِي مَشْيِهِمِ
مُتَشَرِّعِينَ بِشِرْعَةِ الإِيمَانِ

وَهُمُ الَّذِينَ بَنَوا مَنَازِلَ سَيْرِهِمِ
بَيْنَ الرَّجَا وَالخَوفِ لِلدَّيَّانِ

وَهُمُ الَّذِينَ مَلَا الإِلَهُ قُلُوبَهُمُ
بِوِدَادِهِ وَمَحَبَّةِ الرَّحْمَانِ

وَهُمُ الَّذينَ أَكْثَرُوا مِنْ ذِكْرِهِ

في السِّرِّ وَالإِعْلانِ وَالأَحْيانِ

يَتَقَرَّبُونَ إلى المَليكِ بِفِعْلِهِمْ

طاعاتِهِ وَالتَّرْكِ لِلعِصْيانِ

فِعْلُ الفَرائِضِ وَالنَّوافِلِ دَأْبُهُم

مَعَ رُؤْيَةِ التَّقْصيرِ وَالنُّقْصانِ

صَبَرُوا النُّفُوسَ عَلَى المَكارِهِ كُلِّها

شَوقاً إلى ما فيهِ مِنْ إِحْسانِ

نَزَلُوا بِمَنْزِلَةِ الرِّضَى فَهُمْ بِها

قَدْ أَصْبَحُوا في جَنَّةٍ وَأَمانِ

شَكَرُوا الَّذي أَوْلى الخَلائقَ فَضْلَهُ
بِالْقَلْبِ وَالأَقْوالِ وَالأَرْكانِ

صَحِبُوا التَّوَكُّلَ في جَميعِ أُمُورِهِم
مَعَ بَذْلِ جَهْدٍ في رِضَى الرَّحْمانِ

عَبَدُوا الإلهَ عَلى اعْتِقادِ حُضُورِهِ
فَتَبَوَّءُوا في مَنْزِلِ الإحْسانِ

نَصَحُوا الخَليقَةَ في رِضَى مَحْبُوبِهِم
بِالعِلْمِ وَالإرْشادِ وَالإحْسانِ

صَحِبُوا الخَلائقَ بِالجُسُومِ وَإنَّما
أَرْوَاحُهُم في مَنْزِلٍ فَوقانِي

بِاللهِ دَعْواتُ الخَلائِقِ كُلِّها
خَوفاً عَلى الإِيمانِ مِنْ نُقْصانِ

عَزَفُوا القُلُوبَ عَنِ الشَّواغِلِ كُلِّها
قَدْ فَرَّغُوها مِنْ سِوَى الرَّحْمانِ

حَرَكاتُهُم وَهُمُومُهُم وَعُزُومُهُم
للهِ لا لِلْخَلْقِ وَالشَّيْطانِ

نِعْمَ الرَّفِيقُ لِطالِبُ السُّبُلِ الَّتِي
تُفْضِي إِلى الخَيراتِ والإِحْسانِ

TRANSLATION OF THE POEM

Fortunate are those who avoid the destructive paths;
Intending the stations of Allāh's good pleasure.

Those who journey with the utmost sincerity;
Following the legislation by which faith is measured.

Those who build the stations of their journey;
Submitting between being fearful and being hopeful.

Those whose hearts the Divine has filled;
With devotion to Him and love for the Most-Merciful.

Those who remember Him and do so abundantly;
In private, public, at all times in continuance.

Seeking nearness to the Sovereign-Master;
By obeying Him and forsaking disobedience.

Doing what is obligatory and optional is their way;
Inspecting their own faults and their deficiencies.

Their souls patiently enduring all that is disdainful;
Desirous of what it entails of benevolence.

They arrive at the Station of Contentment;
Ultimately reaching the Garden and safety.

For His bounties to His creation they are grateful;
With their heart, tongues and the limbs of their body.

Reliance is their companion in all affairs;
Whilst striving in the pleasure of the All-Merciful.

Worshipping the Divine, believing in His presence;
Thus taking their place at the Station of Excellence.

Advising others to that which pleases their Lord;
With knowledge, guidance and compassion.

Accompanying the people in bodily form;
Whilst their spirits dwell at a sublimer station.

They alert creation to their complete need for Allāh;
Continuously fearing a decrease in their faith.

Their hearts turning away from all distractions;
Completely emptied of other than the Most-Merciful.

Their movements, concerns and their resolves;
Are all for Allāh, not creation, nor the Devil.

The best of friends is the seeker of these paths;
Which leads to acquiring goodness and *iḥsān*.

THE EXQUISITE PEARL

بسم الله الرحمن الرحيم

INTRODUCTION

ALL PRAISE BE TO ALLĀH, Lord of the worlds. May Allāh extol and send blessings and peace upon Muḥammad; and upon his Family, Companions and followers.

These are some brief, but beneficial comments to my poem regarding 'The Journey to Allāh and the Home of the Afterlife;' explaining its meanings and clarifying its premises. The poem encapsulates the main stations (*manāzil*) for the wayfarers to Allāh, which should lead them to the Gardens of Delight and to the closeness of the Munificent Lord. It should also safeguard them from the torment of the Hellfire and from the anguish of being veiled [from Allāh]. I beseech Allāh by His benevolence and bounty that He cause this work to be purely for His Face and for drawing closer to Him.

THE AWAKENING

Realise that what is intended by worship (*'ibādah*) is to serve Allāh, have gnosis (*ma'rifah*) of Him, love Him, continually turn to Him in repentance, and to traverse the paths that lead to the abode of eternal peace (*dār al-salām*).

Most people are overwhelmed by their sensual pleasures and are subjugated by their carnal desires and habits. They give no importance to this matter at all, nor attempt to make it their basis. On the contrary, they turn away from worship and instead pre-occupy themselves with their carnal desires. They abandon it and instead dedicate themselves to their [worldly] pursuits. They do not prevent themselves in order to make up for the time they have squandered. So in their ignorance and oppression they are confused; with their soul's desires they are diverted from being devoted to Allāh; concerning their Lord's remembrance they are heedless; in their religious practice they are remiss; and in the drunken love of their habits they [blindly] wander:

> Those who forgot Allāh, so He caused them to forget their ownselves; such are the corrupt ones. [al-Ḥashr 59:19]

None take heed of this dire neglect and this enormous calamity except for the few who possess intelligence and nobility. They realise that the greatest loss lies in being pre-occupied with that which produces nothing for its doer except perdition and misery. Therefore they prefer the perfect to the imperfect; they trade the ephemeral for the eternal; and they bear the burden of legal responsibility (*taklīf*) and worship until it becomes a source of delight for them and a part of their very nature, by which they become leaders. So listen attentively to their description, and seek the help of Allāh in adorning yourselves with their traits:

THE ASPIRATION

سَعِدَ الَّذِينَ تَجَنَّبُوا سُبُلَ الرَّدَى

وَتَيَمَّمُوا لِمَنَازِلِ الرِّضْوَانِ

1 - Fortunate are those who avoid the destructive paths;
Intending the stations of Allāh's good pleasure.

This is the foundation of their path and the principle course of their party, in that: they avoid the paths of [spiritual] loss and anguish and intend the paths of Allāh's good pleasure. They avoid the paths of Satan and intend to be worshippers of the Most-Merciful. They avoid the paths of the blazing Fire and intend the paths of eternal bliss. They abandon evil and do good. They keep their hearts, tongues and limbs away from prohibited and repugnant actions, and instead busy themselves with obligatory and praiseworthy actions. They adorn themselves with beautiful character and purge themselves of all reprehensible traits.

THE STATION OF SINCERITY

فَهُمُ الَّذِينَ أَخْلَصُوا فِي مَشْيِهِمْ
مُتَشَرِّعِينَ بِشَرْعَةِ الإِيمَانِ

2 - Those who journey with the utmost sincerity;
Following the legislation by which faith is measured.

These two principles, sincerity (*ikhlāṣ*) and conformity (*mutāba'ah*), are a prerequisite for every act of worship, inward or outward, to be valid. Every act that is not done intending the Face of Allāh is futile; and every act that does not conform to the *Sunnah* of Allāh's Messenger *ṣallallāhu 'alayhi wa sallam,* is rejected.[1]

It is only when an action combines sincerity for the One being worshipped - which means intending to seek the Face of Allāh when performing the action - and conformity with the Messenger - by doing

1. Imām Ibn al-Qayyim, may Allāh have mercy upon him, said in *Madārij al-Sālikīn* (2/68): "Allāh said: He Who created death and life, to test which of you are best in action. [al-Mulk 67:2] Fuḍayl ibn 'Iyāḍ said [about this verse]: 'It is what is most sincere and most correct.' They asked: O Abū 'Alī, what is most sincere and most correct? He replied: 'An action, if it is sincere but not correct, will not be accepted. If it is correct but not sincere, it will [also] not be accepted; until it is both sincere and correct. Sincere means that it is exclusively for Allāh, and correct means that it conforms to the *Sunnah.*'"

those actions that have been prescribed and legislated - that an action becomes acceptable.[2]

2. Ibn al-Qayyim, may Allāh have mercy upon him, said in *Madārij al-Sālikīn* (2/70): "It has been said: 'Sincerity is to forget the creation seeing you because of continually looking towards the Creator. Whoever adorns himself before the people with what he does not possess, has fallen from Allāh's grace.' From the words of Fuḍayl are: 'Leaving an action for people's sake is ostentation (*riyā'*), whereas doing an action for people's sake is *shirk*. Sincerity is where Allāh saves you from both of these.' Al-Junayd said: 'Sincerity is a secret (*sirr*) between Allāh and His servant which not even the angel knows so as to record it; nor does Satan know so as to corrupt it; nor is the desire (*hawā*) aware of it so as to influence it.' It was said to Sahl: What is the hardest thing upon the ego (*nafs*)? He replied: 'Sincerity, because the ego has no share of it.'"

Imām Ibn al-Qayyim said about conformity (2/348): "The master of the spiritual faction (*sayyid al-ṭā'ifah*) and their shaykh - Al-Junayd ibn Muḥammad, may Allāh's mercy be upon him - said: 'The paths, all of them are closed to the creation, except for one who emulates the footsteps of the Messenger; may Allāh's blessings and peace be upon him.' He [also]said: 'Whoever does not memorise the Qur'ān nor record the *ḥadīth* should not be followed in this matter, because our science is confined to the Book and the *Sunnah.*' ... Abū Sulaymān al-Dārānī, may Allāh have mercy upon him, said: 'Indeed a word of wisdom occurs to my heart as it does to the nation [of the righteous], but I do not accept it until it is supported by two just witnesses: the Book and the *Sunnah.*'"

THE STATION OF FEAR AND HOPE

وَهُمُ الَّذِينَ بَنَوا مَنازِلَ سَيْرِهِم
بَيْنَ الرَّجا وَالخَوفِ لِلدَّيَّانِ

3 - Those who build the stations of their journey;
Between being fearful and being hopeful.

Meaning that in their journey they attach themselves to reverential fear (*khawf*) and hope (*raja'*) in all their affairs, clinging to them. They do this by inspecting their own faults regarding [the fulfilment of] Allāh's rights, which induces fear in them, and by reflecting upon Allāh's bounties and kindness upon them, which instills hope in them.[3]

They reflect over Allāh's Attributes of greatness, magnificence, wisdom and justice; which induces fear in them, and they reflect upon the Divine Attributes of mercy, munificence, generosity and kindness; having hope in what they necessitate. So when they do an act of goodness, they combine between having fear and hope; hoping for its acceptance,

3. Ibn al-Qayyim, may Allāh have mercy upon him, said (1/390): "The heart, in its journey to Allāh, Majestic is He, is like that of a bird: love is its head, and fear and hope are its two wings. When the head and two wings are sound, the bird flies gracefully; if the head is severed, the bird dies; if the bird loses one of its wings, it then becomes a target for every hunter or predator."

but fearing that it will be rejected. If they do an act of evil, they fear being punished, but hope in being forgiven by the Grace of Allāh.

Between fear and hope they fluctuate; to them they constantly turn to seek shelter; and from them the affairs of their journey alternate. Indeed they are the ones who succeed with flying colours; they are the ones who are victorious.[4]

4. Ibn al-Qayyim, may Allāh sanctify his soul, said (2/27-28) whilst explaining the distinction between true hope and mere wishful thinking *(tamannī)*:

"The difference between it and mere wishful thinking is that mere wishful thinking involves laziness wherein the person neither exerts himself, nor strives [to achieve what he wishes for]. Hope, however, entails striving, exertion and beautiful reliance The first is like the one who wishes that the earth would plant and sow its own seeds for him. The second is like the one who [actually] tills the soil, plants the seeds and then hopes that crops will grow. This is why the gnostics (*'ārifūn*) are agreed that hope is not correct, except if accompanied by action. Shāh al-Kirmānī said: 'The sign of sound hope is good obedience.' And hope is of three types; two are praiseworthy and one type is blameworthy and mere delusion. The first two are the hope of a person who does an act of obedience for Allāh, upon a light from Allāh, hoping in its reward; and like someone who commits a sin, then repents from it, hoping for Allāh's forgiveness, pardon, kindness, magnanimity, clemency and generosity. The third [type] is like a person who persists in sinning and transgressing the limits, yet hopes for Allāh's mercy without doing any action [to warrant it]. This is delusion, mere wishful thinking and false hope."

THE STATION OF LOVE

وَهُمُ الَّذِينَ مَلَا الإِلٰهُ قُلُوبَهُمْ

بِوِدَادِهِ وَمَحَبَّةِ الرَّحْمَانِ

4 - Those whose hearts the Divine has filled;

With devotion to Him and love for the Most-Merciful.

This station - which is the station of love (*maḥabbah*) - is the bedrock of all stations; from it spring every righteous actions, all beneficial deeds and all the lofty stations.[5]

Love refers to the heart being attached to the beloved such that it needs this love and cannot do without it. This requires that the lover withold from all that the Beloved detests and hasten towards all that the Beloved is pleased with, doing so readily, willingly and eagerly. If he speaks, he speaks for Allāh. If he remains silent, he does so for Allāh. If he moves, it is for Allāh. If he remains still, it is for Him. This love then gives rise to a yearning and a restlessness for Allāh, such that the lover never feels settled [unless in His devotion].

5. Ibn al-Qayyim, may Allāh have mercy upon him, said (3/7): "It is the station for which the competitors compete; to it do the workers fix their gaze; for reaching its mark do the forerunners strive; upon it do the lovers annihilate themselves, and with its refreshing breeze do the worshippers revive themselves. It is the heart's strength, the soul's nourishment and the eye's splendour."

If it is said: Does love - which is the highest station - have any causes or means leading to it? It is said in reply: Allāh has not made anything that is sought after, except that He has also made causes and means by which it can be acquired. From the greatest of these causes and means are: withholding from any statement, action or thought that will sever you from it; increasing in the remembrance of Allāh with presence of heart; reflecting upon His noble Word; acknowledging the tremendous bounties that Allāh has bestowed upon the servant; standing before Him with presence of heart and due etiquette; attending the gatherings of the lovers of Allāh; and turning away from whatever will cut you off from any of this. Whoever does this will attain the love of Allāh, if Allāh Wills - and it is His aid that is sought. [6]

This is why I said:

---

6. After mentioning twenty-nine sayings from the gnostics concerning the definition of love, Ibn al-Qayyim, may Allāh have mercy upon him, then said (3/15):

"The thirtieth - which is the most comprehensive of what has been said concerning it. Abū Bakr al-Kattānī said: The topic of love was discussed - may Allāh the Exalted elevate it - during the Pilgrimage season, and all the shaykhs were speaking about it. Al-Junayd was the youngest of them. They said to him: O Iraqi, share with us what you know? So Al-Junayd lowered his head and his eyes filled with tears. He said: 'There is a servant who has left his own soul behind, who is attached to his Lord's remembrance, who is steadfast in fulfilling His rights; who looks to Him with his heart, his heart burning with the lights of His Divine awe. Allāh has purified the draught that he has drunk, from the cup of His Divine love. The All-Mighty has raised for him the veils of the Unseen. When he talks, it is for the sake of Allāh; when he utters, it is about Allāh; when he moves, it is by the command of Allāh; when he is at rest, it is with Allāh. He is for Allāh, by Allāh, with Allāh.' The shaykhs all wept and said: What more can be added to this! May Allāh reward you, O Crown of the Gnostics."

THE STATION OF REMEMBRANCE

وَهُمُ الَّذِينَ أَكْثَرُوا مِنْ ذِكْرِهِ
فِي السِّرِّ وَالإِعْلانِ وَالأَحْيانِ

5 - Those who remember Him and do so abundantly;
In private, public, at all times in continuance.

This is a noble station which each person is in need of; indeed it is a need which ranks above all other needs. The remembrance (*dhikr*) of Allāh is the edifice of one's time. By it grief, anxiety and distress can be dispelled. With it joy and happiness can be obtained. It cultivates barren hearts, makes healthy hearts resplendent, and it leads to the loftiest of stations. In it are benefits and virtues that cannot be enumerated. Allāh, Exalted is He, said:

> O you who believe! Remember Allāh abundantly, and glorify Him morning and evening. [al-Aḥzāb 33:41-42]

The Prophet *ṣallallāhu ʿālayhi wa sallam* advised a man who asked: The duties of Islām are many for me, so instruct me? He replied: "Never let your tongue cease to be moist with the remembrance of Allāh." [7]

7. Reported by at-Tirmidhī (no.3375). It was classified as *ṣaḥīḥ* by Shaykh al-Albānī in *Ṣaḥīḥ al-Jāmiʿ* (no.7700).

He *ṣallallāhu 'ālayhi wa sallam* [also] said: "The loners (*mufarridūn*) lead the way." We asked: Who are the loners? He replied: "Those men and women who remember Allāh abundantly."[8]

I composed the following lines of poetry:

Be one who remembers Allāh under all conditions;
For the remembrance of Allāh has no time restrictions.
The remembrance of the Deity, in private and public;
Will remove your anxiety and grief, and expel it.
Procuring both religious and worldly excellence;
Driving away [evil] whisperings at their occurrence.
The Chosen One informed his Companions one day;
Abundant remembrance is why the loners lead the way.
To seek Allāh's aid was Mu'ādh's given legacy;
So as to remember, thank and worship Him beautifully.
He advised a person who sought sincere council;
Who was striving hard to carry out laws legal.
That let your tongue remain most with it;
This will aid every matter and facilitate it.
He informed that *dhikr* is a plant for its people;
Cultivating Gardens eternal and abodes perpetual.
He informed that Allāh mentions His servant;
And is with him in all matters, facilitating it.
If *dhikr* had no virtue fine;
Except being a path to loving the Divine.
Stopping the youth from backbiting and tale-carrying;
And from uttering that which corrupts their well-being.
A great acquisition and an incentive t'would be;
To engage in Allāh's *dhikr,* abundantly.
But due to our ignorance our *dhikr* is rare;
Just as our worship of the Deity is rare.

8. Reported by Muslim (no.2676).

The *dhikr* of Allāh is a light (*nūr*) for the one remembering Allāh, in his heart, speech, grave, and on the Day of Resurrection. And Allāh's aid is sought.[9]

9. Ibn al-Qayyim, may Allāh have mercy upon him, said in *al-Wābil al-Ṣayyib* (p.63): "I heard Shaykh'l-Islām Ibn Taymiyyah - may Allāh sanctify his soul - say: '*Dhikr* is to the heart as water is to a fish; see what happens to a fish when it is taken out of water!' ... I once attended the morning (*fajr*) Prayer with Shaykh'l-Islām Ibn Taymiyyah, after which he sat down and engaged in *dhikr* of Allāh until it was almost midday. He then turned to me and said: 'This is my morning meal, if I do not partake of it my strength diminishes.'"

SEEKING NEARNESS TO ALLĀH

يَتقرَّبونَ إلى المليك بفعْلهم
طاعاته وَالتَّرْكِ للعصْيان

6 - Seeking nearness to the Sovereign-Master;
By obeying Him and by forsaking disobedience.

Performing these acts of obedience - especially the obligatory ones and leaving the sinful ones - draws one closer to Allāh and leads to Him. In a sacred tradition (*ḥadīth qudsī*) it states: "My servant does not draw closer to Me with anything more beloved to Me, than the obligatory duties that I have enjoined upon him. My servant continues to draw closer to Me by performing optional deeds, until I love him."[10]

Due to this I said:

10. Reported by al-Bukhārī (no.6502).

SELF-INSPECTION

فِعْلُ الفَرَائِضِ وَالنَّوَافِلِ دَأْبُهُمْ
مَعَ رُؤْيَةِ التَّقْصِيرِ وَالنُّقْصَانِ

7 - Doing what is obligatory and optional is their way; Inspecting their own faults and their deficiencies.

Fulfilling the obligatory duties and increasing in performing optional deeds, along with seeing oneself as being deficient or excessive, is from perfection. So striving to do [good] actions eliminates indolence and laziness from oneself, whereas inspecting one's deficiencies dispels the ego's self-conceit (*'ujb*) - which corrupts actions and renders them futile.[11]

11. Ibn al-Qayyim, may Allāh have mercy upon him, said (1/395): "I heard Shaykh'l-Islām Ibn Taymiyyah, may Allāh sanctify his soul, saying: 'The gnostic sees himself as having no right over anyone, nor deems himself as being more virtuous than anyone. This is why he does not reproach, demand or harm.'"

THE STATION OF PATIENCE

صَبَرُوا النُّفُوسَ عَلَى المَكَارِهِ كُلِّهَا

شَوقاً إِلَى مَا فِيهِ مِنْ إِحْسَانِ

8 - Their souls patiently enduring all that is disdainful;

Desirous of what it entails of divine benevolence.

Patient perseverance (*ṣabr*) is restraining the soul from what it finds disdainful, when doing so entails the pleasure of the Most Merciful.[12] Patient perseverance is of three types: patiently persevering in the obedience of Allāh, so that it may be fulfilled; patiently persevering against

12. Ibn al-Qayyim said (2/120): "Al-Junayd said: 'The journey from this world to the Hereafter is smooth and easy for the believer, but leaving ordinary life for the sake of Allāh is difficult. The journey from the ego (*nafs*) to Allāh is extremely difficult, and patience (*ṣabr*) in Allāh is even more difficult.' He was asked about patience, so he replied: 'It is to swallow bitterness without frowning.' Dhu'l-Nūn al-Miṣrī said: 'Patience is to distance yourself from opposing [the truth], to remain calm when engulfed with calamities, and to display sufficiency when poverty occupies your daily life.' It has been said: 'Patience is to face affliction with the best conduct.' It has been said: 'It is to absorb affliction without displaying complaint.' It is said: 'It is accustoming the soul to the onslaught of adversities.' It is said: 'It is to settle down with adversities in good companionship, in the same manner as one settles down with well-being.' And 'Amr ibn 'Uthmān said: 'It is standing firm with Allāh and meeting tribulations with magnanimity and welcome.'"

disobedience, so that it may be abandoned; and patiently persevering with regards to the hardships that Allāh decrees, not showing any impertinence towards it. When the soul feels lazy about obeying Allāh, one exhorts and enjoins it to do so, as well as encouraging it by reminders of the rewards [entailed]. When the soul is strong in inviting towards disobedience to Allāh, one restrains and warns it from doing so, and reminds it about the punishment for disobedience. Patient perseverance is needed in all these affairs.[13]

13. As for complaining in times of adversity, Imām Ibn al-Qayyim, may Allāh have mercy upon him, said in *al-Fawā'id* (pp.130-131):

"The ignorant one complains about Allāh to the people! This is the height of ignorance in complaining and in whom the complaint is about. For if a person were to truly know his Lord, he would never complain of Him? If he truly knew people, he would never complain to them? ... The gnostic complains only to Allāh, and the most knowledgeable of the gnostics are those who complain to Allāh about themselves, not about others ... So there are three levels: The most contemptible of them is to complain to people about Allāh; the loftiest of them is to complain to Allāh about oneself; the middle level is to complain to Allāh about others."

THE STATION OF CONTENTMENT

نَزَلُوا بِمَنْزِلَةِ الرِّضَى فَهُم بِهَا
قَدْ أَصْبَحُوا فِي جَنَّةٍ وَأَمَانِ

9 - They arrive at the Station of Contentment;
Ultimately reaching the Garden and safety.

The station of contentment (*riḍā*) is loftier than that of patience (*ṣabr*). For patience is restraining the soul against what it finds disdainful, although an opposing desire still remains within it. Contentment on the other hand, melts away this opposing desire, causes satisfaction with Allāh and brings about tranquillity and expanse of the breast. It may even cause delight to be experienced in times of hardships, just as others experience delight in times of ease. When the worshippers reaches this station, his life is remedied and his eye experiences coolness. This is why contentment is called: 'a paradise of this world and a repose for the worshippers.'[14]

Whoever is content with Allāh, Allāh is content with him. Whoever is content with simple provisions from Allāh, Allāh is content with simple

14. Ibn al-Qayyim said (2/132): "This is why contentment is one of the greatest gateways to Allāh. It is the paradise of the world, a repose for the gnostics, a life for the lovers, a delight for the worshippers and a coolness of the eye to the yearners."

actions from him. The reality behind contentment is: to receive Allāh's religious ordinances and His All-Embracing Decree with an open heart and a cheerful soul, without resentment or indignation.[15]

15. Ibn al-Qayyim, may Allāh have mercy upon him, said (2/134-135): "Fuḍayl ibn 'Iyāḍ said to Bishr al-Ḥāfī: 'Contentment (*riḍā*) is better than worldly renunciation (*zuhd*), because the one content does not wish for what is above his station.' Abū 'Uthmān was asked about the Prophet *sallallāhu 'alayhi wa sallam's* saying: "I ask You for content after Your Decree." He said: 'This is because being content before the Decree occurs is [actually] the resolve to be content, whereas contentment after it takes place is [true] contentment.' It has been said: 'It is the disappearance of anxiety, whatever the judgement may be.' It is said: 'It is the suspension of preference.' It is said: 'It is to face the judgement with joy.' It has been said: 'It is the heart's tranquillity in the midst of tribulations.' It is said: 'It is the heart looking at Allāh's pre-ordained choice for His servant. It is abandoning resentment.' 'Umar wrote to Abū Mūsā: 'To proceed: Indeed goodness, in its entirety, is encapsulated in contentment; if you are able to be content [then do so], otherwise it is upon you to be patient.' Abū 'Alī al-Daqqāq said: 'The human being is earthenware. Earthenware does not have enough value that it should oppose the judgement of the Truth, Exalted is He.' ... Contentment is of three types: Contentment of the common folk with what Allāh has apportioned and granted; contentment of the elite with what He pre-destined and decreed; contentment of the elite of the elite with Him, to the exclusion of all else besides Him."

THE STATION OF GRATITUDE

شَكَرُوا الَّذِي أَوْلَى الخَلَائِقَ فَضْلَهُ

بِالْقَلْبِ وَالأَقْوَالِ وَالأَرْكَانِ

10 - For His bounties to His creation they are grateful;
With the heart, tongue and the limbs of their body.

Gratitude (*shukr*) is expressed with the heart, by acknowledging Allāh's favours, attesting to them and not considering oneself deserving of them, but instead recognising that they are purely from the Lord's bountiful grace. It is expressed with the tongue by praising Allāh for His favours and proclaiming them. [It is expressed] with the limbs by not being disobedient to Allāh, but rather by utilising His favours to obey Him.[16]

If he is granted any worldly thing, he thanks Allāh for it. If something of this world is removed from him, he [still] thanks Allāh, for sometimes the withdrawal of a favour removes the person from a greater

16. Ibn al-Qayyim, may Allāh have mercy upon him, said (2/186): "Gratitude is built upon five pillars: Submissiveness to Allāh from the one expressing gratitude; loving Him for it; acknowledging His favour; praising Him for it; and not utilising it in a way that displeases Him."

evil. If he is granted the ability to do an act of obedience, he sees this as a grace (*tawfīq*) from Allāh, for which he [again] thanks Him.

And Allāh's aid is sought.

THE STATION OF RELIANCE

صَحِبُوا التَّوَكُّلَ فِي جَمِيعِ أُمُورِهِمْ
مَعَ بَذْلِ جَهْدٍ فِي رِضَى الرَّحْمَانِ

11 - **Reliance is their companion in all affairs;**
Whilst striving in the pleasure of the All-Merciful.

The servant's perfection lies in these two matters, which are: reliance (*tawakkul*) upon Allāh, and striving diligently to obey Allāh. The servant's perfection is hindered by the loss of any one of them.

The reality of reliance entails two matters: dependence upon Allāh and trust in Allāh. So he depends upon his Lord with his heart for procuring what will benefit him, in both his religious and worldly affairs. He acknowledges his lack of power and inability and instead places his trust in Allāh in order to acquire what will benefit him or to repel what will harm him. Futhermore he strives to utilise those causes (*asbāb*) that will lead him to what is sought after.

The details of this is that when he firmly resolves to perform an act of worship, he strives to complete it and beautify it, sparing no effort to do so. He frees himself from depending upon his own self and strength, but instead resorts to, and depends upon, his Lord in order to allow him to complete and perfect [that act]; having a good expectation of Allāh in this and putting his trust in attaining that which he placed his reliance upon Allāh for.

When he firmly resolves to leave an act of disobedience that his soul incites him to, he fulfills those causes that will lead him to leaving that sin; such as considering it and turning his limbs from it. Then, after this, he places his trust in Allāh, resorts to Him in order that He may protect him from it, and has good expectations of Allāh with regards to Allāh protecting him.

If he does this in everything that he does and leaves, then success is to be hoped for him, if Allāh the Exalted wills. But as for the person who seeks Allāh's aid and relies upon Him, but leaves the striving that is a pre-requisite for it, then this is not reliance. Rather, it is mockery! Such is also the case of one who does strive, but depends upon his ownself and does not rely upon his Lord; he is only deluding himself.

THE STATION OF EXCELLENCE

عَبَدُوا الإلَهَ عَلى اعْتِقادِ حُضُورِهِ

فَتَبَوَّءُوا فِي مَنْزِلِ الإحْسَانِ

12 - Worshipping the Divine, believing in His presence; Thus taking their place at the Station of Excellence.

This is the station known as the Station of Excellence (*iḥsān*),[17] which the Prophet *ṣallallāhu ʿālayhi wa sallam* explained as being: "That you worship Allāh as if you see Him, for if you do not see Him, He sees you."[18]

When a person envisages this station in all his states - in particular the state of worship - his heart is prevented from turning to other than his Lord. Instead he is fully content with Allāh, focuses his heart upon Him, and has [spiritual] decorum whilst worshipping Him; doing whatever perfects it and refraining from whatever mars it. This station is one of the greatest and sublimest of all spiritual stations. However it requires

17. Imām Ibn al-Qayyim said about *iḥsān* (2/344): "It is the quintessence (*lubb*) of faith as well as its spirit and perfection. This station contains all other stations; it embodies them all and they are enveloped by it."

18. Reported by al-Bukhārī (no.5) and Muslim (no.9).

gradually training the souls, step-by-step. The servant will not cease habituating his soul to it until he is drawn to it and accustoms himself with it. Then the servant will live in delight of his Lord, experiencing joy and bliss in His closeness.[19]

19. To worship Allāh whilst being aware of His Ever-Watchful Presence is also known as the Station of Vigilance (*murāqabah*), about which Ibn al-Qayyim, may Allāh have mercy upon him, said (2/50):

"Al-Junayd said: 'If someone actualises vigilance, he will fear losing even a second from his Lord, and nothing else.' Dhu'l-Nūn said: 'The sign of vigilance is to prefer what Allāh revealed, to magnify what Allah magnified, and to debase what Allāh debased.' It has been said: 'Hope moves you to acts of obedience; fear removes you from acts of disobedience; and vigilance begets to you the path of realities.' It was said: 'Vigilance is watching over the heart because of realising the Truth's gaze with every thought and step.' ... It was said: 'The best of what a person can attach himself to in this Path is: to call oneself to account, vigilance, and governance of one's actions through knowledge.' Abū Ḥafs said to Abū 'Uthmān al-Naysābūrī: 'When you preach to people, be an exhorter (*wāʿiẓ*) to your own heart and soul. In that way you will not be deceived by their gathering around you; for they are observing your exterior, but Allāh is observing your interior.'"

THE STATION OF GOOD CHARACTER

نَصَحُوا الخَلِيقَةَ فِي رِضَى مَحْبُوبِهِم

بِالعِلْمِ وَالإِرْشَادِ وَالإِحْسَانِ

13 - **Advising others to that which pleases their Lord;**
With knowledge, guidance and compassion.

صَحِبُوا الخَلائِقَ بِالجُسُومِ وَإِنَّمَا

أَرْوَاحُهُم فِي مَنْزِلٍ فَوقَانِي

14 - **Accompanying the people in bodily form;**
Whilst their spirits dwell at a sublimer station.

This is their state with the people, which is the most perfect of states and the sublimest.

They begin by sincerely advising people to their utmost, loving for them the good they love for themselves; deploring for them the evil they deplore for themselves; striving to remove every evil from them with all that is possible; and exerting themselves in order to bring about benefit to them with every means at their disposal. [This they do] by enjoining goodness, forbidding evil, feeding those that suffer from hunger, clothing those that are destitute, alliviating those that are distressed, teaching those that are ignorant, restraining those that are oppressors, helping those that are oppressed, warding-off potential harm from people, and keeping the harms of their ownselves away from others. Furthermore, their association with people is external and bodily; as for their hearts and spirits, they hover around the Beloved and seek to be as close to Him as possible.[20]

Sometimes the person humbly abases himself before Him, with fear and humility. Furthermore, he expresses gratitude to Him through love of Him; being led to this by witnessing His kindness and closeness. He then inclines towards all that is pleasing to Allāh, strives in the worship of Him and shows benevolence to His creation. Indeed these are the [true] people; these are the intelligent and perspicuous ones. And there is no might, nor power, except with Allāh.

20. Ibn al-Qayyim said (2/248): "Good character with the Creator and with the creation revolves around two statements which were mentioned by Shaykh 'Abd al-Qādir al-Jīlānī who said: 'Be with the Truth, without creation; and be with creation, without ego (*nafs*).' So consider carefully! How amazing are these statements, despite their brevity, and how they gather together the principles of wayfaring (*sulūk*) and every beautiful character. Corruption of character arises from putting the creation between yourself and Allāh, and by putting your ego between yourself and His creation. So when you isolate the creation, in that state when you are with Allāh the Exalted; and when you isolate your ego, in that state when you are with the creation - then you have fully attained to the ideals of the People of Spirituality (*al-qawm*). And Allāh's aid is sought."

THE STATION OF ATTENTIVE CARE

بِاللهِ دَعْوَاتُ الخَلَائِقِ كُلِّهَا
خَوفاً عَلَى الإِيمَانِ مِنْ نُقْصَانِ

15 - **They alert creation to their complete need for Allāh;**
Continuously fearing a decrease in their faith.

This is the Station of Attentive Care (*riʿāyah*) of the realities of faith and of the milestone of *iḥsān.* For it is not befitting for the worshipper to ever turn away from contemplating his own condition and reflecting upon the deficiencies in his own actions. Instead he should expend all his efforts - before, as well as whilst, performing an action - in making sure that it is performed correctly and excellently. He should also safeguard it from anything that may render it void, and remove from it anything that may corrupt it. For indeed, preserving the action is actually greater than the action itself. Thus, whenever a person increases in his attentive care and increases in his striving in the action, his faith increase. If, however, his attentive care decreases, his faith diminishes in proportion.

From the greatest of matters wherein attentive care should be exercised is in performance of actions, and in the milestone of *iḥsān;* which refers to the fervent desire to perform acts of worship with presence of heart and total devotion to Allāh.

Likewise, from the most important matters that deserve attentive care are the favours of Allah that He bestows upon a person. It is desired for a person to greatly thank Allāh for granting him the grace to perform that action.

Likewise, [from those matters that deserve] attentive care is fear and hope; fearing that the act may be rejected due to self-conceit (*'ujb*), ostentation (*riyā'*), arrogance (*takabbur*), or by not fulfilling it in the way that it deserves to be fulfiled; yet hoping in its acceptance by Allāh's mercy, benevolence and grace - which includes being granted the grace to perform that action in the first place.

THE STATION OF RENUNCIATION

عَزَفُوا الْقُلُوبَ عَنِ الشَّوَاغِلِ كُلِّهَا

قَدْ فَرَّغُوهَا مِنْ سِوَى الرَّحْمَانِ

16 - Their hearts turning away from all distractions;

Completely emptied of other than the Most-Merciful.

حَرَكَاتُهُمْ وَهُمُومُهُمْ وَعُزُومُهُمْ

لِلَّهِ لَا لِلْخَلْقِ وَالشَّيْطَانِ

17 - Their movements, concerns and their resolves;

Are all for Allāh, not creation, nor the Devil.

Meaning that they empty their hearts of all that distracts them from Allāh and distances them from His good pleasure; this being the reality of worldly renunciation (*zuhd*).[22]

22. Ibn al-Qayyim, may Allāh have mercy upon him, said: (2/11): "Imām Aḥmad bin Ḥanbal said: '*Zuhd* is of three degrees: Firstly, to avoid the forbidden; this is the *zuhd* of the common people. Secondly, to avoid what is lawful but unnecessary; this is the *zuhd* of the elite. Thirdly, to avoid everything that distracts one from Allāh; this is the *zuhd* of the gnostics.'."

This emptying will not be sufficient until and unless the heart is filled with beneficial thoughts and truthful resolves. So the servant's ideas and thoughts should be concerned with all that will draw him closer to Allāh; such as acquiring knowledge, contemplating over the Qur'ān, remembering Allāh with presence of heart, reflecting over Allāh's kindness, the fear of slipping and committing disobedience, reflecting over the Attributes of the All-Merciful and the fact that they are free from every blemish and defect, and reflecting upon the grave and its states; the Day of Resurrection and its events; Paradise and its delights; and Hell and its blazing fire.

Their thoughts revolve around these matters, away from those negative thoughts that engender nothing but grief, harm, wasting of time and psychological instability; all of which are unhealthy for a person, both in this life and the Afterlife.[23]

23. After having discussed four types of thoughts and reflections - reflecting over the Qur'ān, the creation, Allāh's bounties, and the blemishes of one's own soul and actions - that are vital to a person's psycho-spiritual growth, Ibn al-Qayyim then said in *al-Dā' wa'l-Dawā'* (p.239):

"The Fifth: Reflecting upon the obligation of the moment and its duty, and to then firmly resolve to fulfil it. So the gnostic is, 'the son of his moment.' If he loses it, he loses all of its benefits. For all benefits arise from the moment, if you lose it you will never again be able to reach it. Al-Shāfi'ī, may Allāh be pleased with him, said: 'I accompanied the *Ṣūfīs* and I did not benefit from them other than for two words. One was their saying: Time is like a sword, if you do not cut it, it will cut you.' He mentioned the other saying [as being]: 'Your soul, if it is not kept busy with the Truth, it will busy you with falsehood.' "

THE FELLOWSHIP

نِعْمَ الرَّفِيقُ لِطَالِبُ السُّبُلِ الَّتِي

تُفْضِي إِلَى الخَيْرَاتِ وَالإِحْسَانِ

18 - The best of friends is the seeker of these paths;
Which leads to acquiring goodness and *iḥsān.*

These are the ones who will cause their friends to be happy, providing they follow their path. Theirs is the path that Allāh has ordered we ask Him to guide us to, because of Him favouring them with true faith and with actualising it.

We ask Allāh that He guides us to the Straight Path, the path of those whom He has bestowed His grace:

> Of the Prophets, the truthful ones, the martyrs and the pious; they are the best of company. [al-Nisā' 4:69]

We ask that He save us from the paths of His anger and misguidance, which lead to disgrace and destruction, for He is the most generous of those who show generosity and the most merciful of those who show mercy. I ask Allāh - seeking the means of nearness to Him by His most beautiful Names, Attributes and Favours - that He not prevent us from the good that is with Him of Divine benevolence and forgiveness, because of our evils, our deficiencies in fulfilling His rights and our transgressions; and that He makes this sincerely for seeking His Face and a cause for attaining bliss in the Gardens of Paradise.

May Allāh shower abundant blessings and peace upon Muḥammad, the unlettered Prophet, who was sent as a mercy to the worlds; and upon his Family, Companions and followers.

TRANSLATOR'S BIBLIOGRAPHY

AL-ALBĀNĪ, Muḥammad Nāsir al-Dīn. *Ṣaḥīḥ al-Jāmiʿ al-Saghīr wa Ziyādah.* Beirut: Maktabah al-Islāmī, 1406H.

Silsilah al-Aḥādīth al-Ṣaḥīḥah. Riyadh: Maktabah al-Maʿārif, 1407H.

AL-ʿASQALĀNĪ, Ibn Ḥajr. *Fatḥ al-Bārī Sharḥ Ṣaḥīḥ al-Bukhārī.* Beirut: Dār Kutub al-ʿIlmiyyah, 1410H.

AL-BAGHAWĪ, al-Ḥusayn ibn Masʿūd. *Maʿālim al-Tanzīl.* Riyadh: Dār Ṭayyibah, 1417H.

IBN ḤANBAL, Aḥmad bin Muḥammad. *Al-Musnad.* Beirut: Mu'assasah al-Risālah, 1421H.

IBN QAYYIM AL-JAWZIYYAH, Shams al-Dīn Muḥammad. *Al-Dā' wa'l-Dawā'.* Riyadh: Dār Ibn al-Jawzī, 1419H.

Al-Fawā'id. Beirut: Dār al-Kitāb al-ʿArabī, 1413H.

Madārij al-Sālikīn. Beirut: Dār Iḥyā al-Turāth al-ʿArabī, 1419H.

Al-Wābil al-Ṣayyib. Cairo: Dār al-Rayyān li'l-Turāth, 1408H.

IBN RAJAB, Zayn al-Dīn Abu'l-Faraj. *Jāmiʿ al-Ūlūm wa'l-Ḥikam.* Beirut: Mu'assasah al-Risālah, 1419H.

IBN TAYMIYYAH, Taqī al-Dīn Aḥmad. *Majmūʿ Fatāwā.* Riyadh: Dār ʿĀlam al-Kutub, 1411H.

AL-MUBĀRAKFŪRĪ, Muḥammad ʿAbd al-Raḥmān. *Tuḥfat al-Aḥwadhī bi Sharḥ Jāmiʿ al-Tirmidhī.* Beirut: Dār Kutub al-ʿIlmiyyah, 1410H.

AL-NAWAWĪ, Yaḥyā ibn Sharaf. *Ṣaḥīḥ Muslim bi Sharḥ al-Nawawī.* Beirut: Dār al-Kutub al-ʿIlmiyyah, 1415H.

AL-RAMYĀN, ʿAbd Allāh. *Al-Juhūd al-Da'awiyyah wa'l-ʿIlmiyyah li'l-Shaykh ʿAbd al-Raḥmān al-Saʿdī.* Riyadh: Dār Muslim, 1419H.

AL-SAMʿĀNĪ, Abu'l-Muzaffar. *Tafsīr al-Qur'ān.* Riyadh: Dār al-Waṭn, 1418H.

AL-ṬABARĪ, Ibn Jarīr. *Jāmiʿ al-Bayān ʿan Ta'wīl al-Qur'ān.* Beirut: Dār Kutub al-ʿIlmiyyah, 1412H.

GENERAL INDEX

ʿAbd al-ʿAzīz bin Bāz, xvi
ʿAbd Allāh ibn ʿĀʾid al-Ḥarbī, xvi
ʿAbd al-Qādir al-Jīlānī, 27
ʿAlī ibn Nāṣir Abū Wādī, xvi
ʿAmr ibn ʿUthmān, 16
Abū ʿAlī al-Daqqāq, 19
Abū Bakr al-Kattānī, 10
Abū Ḥafs, 25
Abū Hurayrah, viii
Abū Mūsā, 19
Abū Sulaymān al-Dārānī, 6
Abū ʿUthmān al-Naysābūrī, 25
advising, 26
Afterlife (*ākhirah*), v, vii, x, xiii, xiv
Aḥmad bin Ḥanbal, 12
al-Albānī, vii, 12
altruist, xii
angelic, viii
arrogance (*takabbur*), 29
aspirant, vi
aspiration (*irādah*), vi, vii, 4
attentive care (*riʿāyah*), 28, 29
authorization (*ʿijāzah*), xvi
awakening, x, 2
al-Azhar, xvi

al-Baghawī, xiv
Banū Tamīm, xv
bestial, viii
beautific vision, xiv
Bishr al-Ḥāfī, 19

capriciousness (*hawā*), x
causes (*asbāb*), 17
character, 26, 27
contentment (*riḍā*), 18, 19
Creator, v, 6, 27

Day of Resurrection, v, 13, 31
Decree, 19
delight, xii, xiii, xiv, 1, 18, 25
dhikr, 11, 12, 13
Dhu'l-Nūn al-Miṣrī, 16, 25
duties, xi, 11

ego (*nafs*), x, xii, 6, 15, 27
environmental vandalism, vi
eye of spiritual perception, xi
exhorter (*wāʿiẓ*), xvi, 25
existentialism, vi
expansion, xiii

Face [of Allāh], xiv, 1, 5, 33
faith (*īmān*), vi, viii, ix, x, xii, 28
fear (*khawf*), viii, xi, 7, 27, 29, 31
fiqh, xvi, xvii

Fire, 4
flashes (*bawāriq*), xviii
al-Fuḍayl ibn 'Iyāḍ, 5, 6, 19
fellowship, 32

Gardens of Delight, 1
gazing, xiv
generosity, 7,8
glimmerings, xvii, xix
gnosis, xi, xii, 2
gnostic (*'ārif*), ix, 8, 10, 15, 17, 31
goodness, 7
Grace [of Allāh], 6, 8, 20, 29
gratitude, 20
greatness, 7

ḥadīth, xvi, 6
Ḥamad, xv
Ḥanbalī, viii, xvii
hedonism, vi
Hellfire, 1
Hijāz, xvi
hope (*rajā*), xix, 7, 8
humanity, v, vi
humility, 27
hunger, 27

Ibn al-Qayyim, viii, x, xiii, 5, 6, 7, 8, 9, 10, 13, 15, 16, 17, 18, 19, 20, 24, 25, 27, 30, 31
Ibn Qayyim al-Jawziyyah, *see above*
Ibn Rajab al-Ḥanbalī, viii, ix, xi
Ibn Taymiyyah, viii, xi, xii, xiii, xvii, 13, 15
ideology, vi
iḥsān, viii, xi, xxvii, 24, 28
inner struggle (*mujāhadah*), vi, x, xx
intimacy, xi, xiii

al-Junayd, 6, 10, 16, 25
jurisprudence (*fiqh*), xvi
jihād, x

knowledge, xvi, xvii, xix, xxvii, 25, 31

liberalism, v
love (*maḥabbah*), xi, xii, xviii, 8, 9, 10, 12, 14, 20, 25, 27
lovers of Allāh, xiii, 9, 10, 18

maḥabbah, 9
mass consumerism, vi
materialism, vi, xix
muḥaddith, xvi
mujāhadah, xx
murāqabah, 25

nation (*ummah*), xix, 6
nihilism, vi

Ones Brought Near (*muqarrabūn*), xi
oppression, 2, 27
orator (*khaṭīb*), xvi
ostentation (*riyā'*), 6, 29

Paradise, x, xiii, xiv, 18, 31, 33
patience (*ṣabr*), xviii, xix, 16, 17
peace, 2
perdition, 2
pietists, xx
Pious Predecessors, xix
poverty, vii, 16

promise, xiv, xxi
psychological instability, 37
psychosis, vi

quintessence (*lubb*), 24
Qur'ān, xv, xvii, 31

ranks, xviii
reflecting, 7, 31
reliance, xix, xxvii, 8, 22, 23
remembrance (*dhikr*), xiii, 2, 8, 10, 11, 12, 31
renunciation (*zuhd*), xviii, xix, 19, 30
repentance, 2
reward, xii, 8, 10, 17
reverence, xi
reverential fear (*khawf*), 7, 27
Righteous (*abrār*), xi, xvii

Sacred Law (*sharīʿah*), viii, x, xv
Satan, 4, 6
scrupulousness, xv
self-inspection, 15
self-conceit (*ʿujb*), 15, 29
servitude (*ʿubūdiyyah*), xii
al-Shāfiʿī, 31
Shah al-Kirmānī, 8
shirk, 6
sincerity (*ikhlāṣ*), ix, xviii, 8, 12, 15, 22, 23, 27
soul, xiii, xix, xx, xxvi, 2, 16, 22
spirituality, vi
spiritual diseases, viii
spiritual growth, xxi
spiritual perception, viii, ix, x, xi
spiritual tradition, viii
state (*ḥāl*), xviii, xix
station (*maqām*), ix, xviii, xix, xx, xxvi, xxvii, 1, 4, 5, 7, 9, 10, 16, 18, 19, 20, 22, 24, 26, 28, 30
striving, x, xxvii, 8, 12, 15, 22, 23, 27
ṣūfī, 31
sulūk, xvii, xviii, xix, xx, 17
Sunnah, xix, 5, 6
sweetness, xii, xiii

taste [of faith], xii
tongues, xxvii, 4
tranquil, xiii, 19
Truthful Ones (*siddīqūn*), xviii

ummah, xix

veil, xiv, 1, 10
victorious, 8
vigilance (*murāqabah*), ix, xi, 25
vision, xiv

wayfarer, xx, 1, 2
wayfaring, x, xi,
wisdom, 6
witnessing (*mushāhadah*), ix, x, xi, xiii, 27
world (*dunyā*), x, xiii, xiv, xx, xxi, 1, 22
worldliness, vii, xvi, xix
worship, viii, ix, xiv, xvi, xxvii, 1, 2, 3, 5, 12, 13, 22, 24, 27, 28

yearning, x, xi, xiii, 9, 18